Praying Through Our Losses

MEDITATIONS FOR THOSE WHO ARE GRIEVING

Wayne Simsic

the WORD among us®
press

The Word Among Us Press
Copyright © 2007 by Wayne Simsic

Portions published in 1994 under the title *Cries of the Heart: Praying Our Losses* by Saint Mary's Press, 702 Terrace Heights, Winona, MN 55987-1320.

The Word Among Us Press
7115 Guilford Drive
Frederick, Maryland 21704
www.wau.org

16 15 14 13 12   4 5 6 7 8

ISBN: 978-1-59325-098-0

Cover design by Laura Steur-Alvarez

Made and printed in the United States of America

Library of Congress Cataloging-in-Publication Data

Simsic, Wayne.
  Praying through our losses : meditations for those who are grieving / Wayne Simsic.
      p. cm.
  ISBN 978-1-59325-098-0 (alk. paper)
1. Consolation. 2. Grief--Religious aspects--Christianity--Meditations.
3. Loss (Psychology)--Religious aspects--Christianity--Meditations. I. Title.
  BV4905.3.S576 2007
  242'.4--dc22
                              2006101975

May those who sow in tears
reap with shouts of joy.
—Psalm 126:5

Contents

Introduction

To Those Who Have Experienced a Loss

This book of prayers is for those who are actively grieving and for those who are confronting past losses. These prayers are written to help you face grief issues like shock, denial, depression, anger, and the wide range of grief responses common to all losses. They provide words that you may need when your heart is still preoccupied with the painful effects of loss, regardless of when the loss occurred.

Death is certainly the most obvious type of loss, but it is not the only kind. We may lose our health, relationships, fertility, jobs, money, self-esteem, youth, reputation, sense of security, a cherished goal, or dreams of the future. Life transitions that we take for granted, like moving to a new home, involve a painful letting go that cannot easily be dismissed. Letting go of anyone or anything we cherish hurts. For example, since September 11 we have lost a sense of security and are reminded of this almost daily by media reports of terrorist activities throughout the world.

Each loss is personal and unique. Another person cannot fully enter our pain and understand it. Yet in many ways, all people go through the same process, because we are all part of the human community. Thus, we can help each other in our grieving, because we journey together.

What Is Grief?

Grief is the painful process of adjusting to a loss. No matter how much inner strength we may have or how strong our faith may be, we are destined to grieve. Even though God delivered the people of the Exodus from slavery, they grieved and had to face the hardship of the wilderness before they found the promised land. They experienced brokenness before realizing that God traveled with them every step of the way. Grieving is a kind of exodus. We get lost in the desert of our suffering and want to turn back. Nevertheless, the God who journeys with us can lead the way out of the desert and into a fertile land.

If someone dies, someone whose soul has been linked to our own, our grief can be overwhelming. When a friend and mentor of mine died of cancer, I didn't grieve for him at the time. Months later I picked up a book he had written. When I saw his name and recalled how he had helped others through his teaching, the emotions that had been carefully stored in a dark corner of my heart broke free, and I wept. Later, upon reflection, I felt that this spontaneous expression of grief opened me to the grieving process and simultaneously honored the gift of the relationship.

Grief is not a hurdle that we can jump over at will or a barrier that we can avoid if we are careful. After his wife's death from cancer, C. S. Lewis recognized the all-encompassing reality of grief: "Her absence is like the sky, spread over everything" (*A Grief Observed*). On our way toward the light, healthy grieving leads us through the darkness and transforms us. Whether our loss is great or small, we must grieve it if we are to move on to new life.

We may find ourselves mourning the victims of tragedies like the Rwanda genocide, September 11, hurricane Katrina, or a devastating tsunami or earthquake. Through the media, we are constantly exposed to disasters throughout our global and local communities that break open our hearts and bow our heads in sorrow. As I write these paragraphs, my local newspaper reports people killed in Iraq, the drowning of a boy in a nearby lake, and fears of a Somalia conflict. We feel helpless as we mourn these losses, perhaps saying a spontaneous prayer for those who have suffered or died.

However, can we really grieve all these tragedies without being overwhelmed by the sheer weight of human pain? The answer is that, even though the events themselves are out of our hands, we, as Christians, should take suffering to heart as much as we are capable and mourn the losses of other people, the planet earth, and all creation. We grieve not as people who somehow stand apart from a particular tragedy, but with the conviction of our oneness with the human family and with all creation, and with an awareness of our call to feel the sufferings and needs of others as our own.

In general, although we have little choice about the losses that life inevitably brings us, we can choose how we will respond to them. We can ignore the losses that enter our lives, masking or burying our suffering, or we can take time to enter our feelings, own the changes that losses bring about in us, and ask for help from other people and from God.

Our culture tempts us to ignore grief; to escape through work, drink, sleep, or frenzied activity. However, if we do not grieve, we create a barrier between ourselves and others as well as between ourselves and God; and, inevitably, the woundedness and pain we so desperately try to ignore will resurface each time we encounter a new loss.

How Do We Deal with a Loss?

Grieving generally follows four broad movements. In the first phase, we acknowledge our loss. We enter this phase when we experience shock, confusion, disbelief, and other emotions that immediately follow a loss. In the second phase, we struggle with what the loss means to us; feelings and thoughts surface unexpectedly, causing enormous pain. In this stage we need to express our feelings and tell our story repeatedly. The more detail we use in expressing the pain, the easier it is to cope.

Eventually, we enter a phase of healing and hope, a place where joy becomes part of our lives again. We realize that we will survive the loss, and we can begin to let go of our grief. And finally, in the fourth phase, we make the choice to move forward into a new life. There are still days of sadness but, for the most part, we can see progress. It is not as if we have forgotten a loved one or no longer care, only that we have progressed enough in our grief journey to see a light shine through the darkness. In the process, the loved one has found a home deep in our heart and become a part of our lives, influencing us in intimate and surprising ways.

These stages provide guidelines, but the grieving process cannot be restricted to any neat pattern of behavior. The movements of grieving overlap. One phase may be more difficult than the others and take longer to navigate. We do not all move through the phases in the same way or at the same speed. There are no deadlines for the transition through a loss. Instead, the grieving process is unique to us and our situation.

One element that is common to all grief is the need for spiritual resources. Grief may introduce us to the most intimate and sacred journey that we could imagine. As we search for answers in our grief and wrestle with strong feelings, we find ourselves at the center of our spirituality. Like Job, we need to discover our faith again, this time from the perspective of a heart in agony. The wounded heart cries out for help. This cry becomes a spontaneous prayer throughout the day. When our own words fail us, we can turn to the biblical psalms, music, favorite poems, or quotes from books.

The prayers in this book focus on the psalms as a primary resource in times of suffering. Psalms that deal with suffering or loss originate in the heart of the psalmist and, therefore, in an uncanny way, echo our own cry of anguish, our own anger, bitterness, doubt, and despair. Praying the psalms affords us words when all we can bear is silence. The psalms ring true because they lament honestly and forcefully; they are never sentimental or understated. However, more importantly, they not only express our deepest feelings but return us to the source of healing: God. In the psalms we find that God has accompanied us all along in our suffering.

The painful process of grieving urges us to rely on God, echoing the gospel message to trust in the divine and surrender to a power greater than ourselves. Even in the bleakest times, God

remains near, gently inviting us to hand over our life to infi-
nite love. This love will never abandon us; it reveals itself most
dramatically in those people who sensitively mediate love for
us. The process of grieving teaches a simple lesson: the journey
from sorrow to peace and from anger to harmony cannot be
made in isolation.

How to Use These Prayers

Although the prayers that follow are grouped according to
the four stages of grieving, they do not have to be used in any
particular order. You are likely to identify with some prayers
more than others. Use the prayers that speak most strongly to
you when you need them.

At the beginning of each prayer, pause and place yourself in
God's loving presence. Get in touch with your feelings of pain,
loneliness, despair, anger, love, or hope. Pray slowly. Let the
meaning of the words take shape for you. You may want to
include other prayers, readings, silent pauses, or dialog with God
as you go along. You might read the prayers in the company of
books like Henri Nouwen's *In Memoriam* or C. S. Lewis' *A
Grief Observed*. Whatever way you choose, listen to your heart
and let these prayers reinforce your ongoing cry to God.

You may also feel the desire to keep a journal. Since grief
is neither an illness nor a pathological condition, but rather a
highly personal and normal response to life-changing events that
can lead to healing and inner growth, you might find support in
the process of writing out your feelings. For example, you may
follow your reading of a particular prayer with some time to

express on paper the feelings that the prayer released in you.

One healing exercise for many is to tell the story of your loss; for example, your relationship with the deceased. Write about the events preceding the loss, special times or memories that surrounded the loss, decisions that had to be made, and the influence of certain people. There may be events or images that you cannot get out of your head or things you wish you had done differently. Tell the story in narrative form and describe any feelings that arise. Cry, express anger if necessary; and, later, if you feel the need, share the story with someone else.

Here are a few more suggestions to survive a time of loss:

- **Make a commitment to the grieving process.** Spend at least fifteen minutes a day praying, walking, performing different rituals, or just remaining silent.

- **Practice deep, slow, meditative breathing.** Slowly inhale and exhale; it may help to repeat a short phrase to yourself, like "God be with me" or "Jesus, healer."

- **Take time to rest.** The grief process is exhausting. In many cases this may be your form of prayer.

- **Accept support and care from friends and family.** Be open especially to those who have experienced a similar loss.

- **Practice meditation.** Meditation can involve any activity that calms the mind, like jogging, walking, dancing, reading Scripture, listening to music, or concentration on breathing.

- **Be a friend to yourself.** Don't take on unnecessary challenges and responsibilities. They will only drain you and distract your attention from the task of grieving.

- **Accept your feelings.** Let guilt, anger, and depression enter your prayer. Bring your entire self before God just like the psalmists did.

- **Keep a journal.** See comments above. Writing helps you acknowledge and honor your thoughts and emotions, and thus provides a way to work through them. Do not force yourself to write, but do so when you feel the need. Writing can become a way of praying.

- **Laugh.** Laughter may be a healing form of prayer. Humor allows us to respond more humanly to our loss.

- **Forgive yourself, and forgive the other person.** Put yourself in the presence of God's love and let go of any shortcomings, harsh words, unexpressed feelings, actions not performed, and mistakes you or the other person may have made. Without forgiveness, we will not be open to God's healing love.

- **Honor your own experience and the experience of others who grieve.** Don't expect yourself to be at a particular stage at any particular time, but allow yourself the time and the emotions that you need.

- **Above all, be assured that you will heal.** You will feel better. God is not far away. You only have to ask for help, and you will realize that love was present all along, waiting for you to reach out and embrace it.

In the belief that we can be healed, let us pray using the words of the psalmist:

Give ear to my prayer, O God;
    do not hide yourself from my supplication.
Attend to me, and answer me;
    I am troubled in my complaint.
I am distraught. . . .
My heart is in anguish within me,
    the terrors of death have fallen upon me.
Fear and trembling come upon me,
    and horror overwhelms me.
And I say, "O that I had wings like a dove!
    I would fly away and be at rest."
—Psalm 55:1-2, 4-6

May you find strength and healing in the prayers that follow and perseverance in the ongoing journey of your grief—and eventually find freedom from your sadness and sorrow in the embrace of a loving God.

PART 1
ACKNOWLEDGING LOSS

*To pass through our grief,
we must first face the truth
that someone or something we love is gone.*

For he has said: "I will never leave you or forsake you."
—Hebrews 13:5

SHOCK

Opening: O God, I am shattered; my heart lies open and wounded. One moment everything was ordinary, secure. Then suddenly my life was on the edge of an abyss, and I was falling. Time has stopped, and nothing seems important anymore. I don't care to eat. People walk by me as if everything is normal, not realizing that my heart is being torn apart.

Psalm

O Lord, God of my salvation,
    when, at night, I cry out in your presence,
let my prayer come before you;
    incline your ear to my cry.

For my soul is full of troubles,
    and my life draws near to Sheol.
I am counted among those who go down to the Pit;
    I am like those who have no help,
like those forsaken among the dead,
    like the slain that lie in the grave,
like those whom you remember no more,
    for they are cut off from your hand.
You have put me in the depths of the Pit,
    in the regions dark and deep.
—Psalm 88:1-6

Reflection

Our first tendency is to escape the shock of grief and get on with our life, but grief will not just disappear. It insists on taking its course and smashing us down like a tidal wave.

We live through the shock, stumbling through life day by day, reading sentences without concentrating, and staring out windows in a daze. Shock serves as the initial line of defense that enables us to carry on under overwhelming sorrow. It is a temporary escape that prepares us for the next stage of grief.

Rather than ignore shock, perhaps we should take time to pour out our feelings in a letter, in a mournful song, or in a lamentation prayer to the person or thing lost.

Hymn

Cry aloud, then, to God,
let your tears flow like a torrent,
    day and night;
give yourself no relief,
    grant your eyes no rest.
—Adapted from Lamentations 2:18

Closing: O God, the loneliness I feel has no language, only a cry. My heart has filled with sorrow. I am beyond help. Day and night I raise my voice to you, hoping for an answer. Hear my plea, O God, and do not abandon me. The wound in my heart will not heal.

The Pain of Grief

Opening: Merciful God, I am confused, lonely, and sad. I do not feel like talking with people. Emotions drain my strength, leaving me numb and hopeless. Tears well up at unexpected times. What am I to do, O God? I have no control. Give me the strength to bear these bitter tears.

Psalm

As a deer longs for flowing streams,
    so my soul longs for you, O God. . . .
My tears have been my food
    day and night,
while people say to me continually,
    "Where is your God?" . . .
Why are you cast down, O my soul,
    and why are you disquieted within me?
Hope in God; for I shall again praise him,
    my help and my God.
—Psalm 42:1, 3, 5-6

Reflection

Grief rushes in, abates for a time, then rushes in again. The immense pain takes away words. We receive news that a friend has died, that we have a chronic illness, that we have lost our job, or that we have sustained some other loss. Dreadful images storm our imagination. Yet we cannot dismiss the pain. Any attempt to do so only intensifies the anguish.

We carry the weight of grief from month to month, until we are finally willing to let go. None of this is controlled. Feelings of denial, anger, and the harsh reality of pain rule our life. Jesus wept during his prayer at Gethsemane and said to his followers, "My soul is sorrowful to the point of death" (adapted from Matthew 26:38). In our suffering, we repeat the same words and try to find in them not weakness but transformation.

Hymn

> I am the one familiar with misery
>   under the rod of God's anger;
> I am the one God has forced to walk
>   in darkness, and without any light.
> God holds up a hand against me alone,
>   again and again, all day long.
> **—Adapted from Lamentations 3:1-3**

Closing: Give me the strength, merciful God, to pass through my pain, and let it transform my soul. Teach me to express my grief honestly, to cry, and to weather the onslaught of emotions while trusting in you.

No Relief

Opening: Faithful God, I am unable to find comfort in anything—in well-meaning friends who try to console me, in Scripture, and even in you.

PSALM

How long, O LORD? Will you forget me forever?
   How long will you hide your face from me?
How long must I bear pain in my soul,
   and have sorrow in my heart all day long? . . .
Consider and answer me, O LORD my God!
   Give light to my eyes, or I will sleep the sleep of death.
—Psalm 13:1-2, 3

REFLECTION

In the early stages of grief, we find ourselves inconsolable. We don't want to hear the well-intentioned words of friends and even wonder whether they know our pain is real or whether they realize how little they can do to comfort us. We may be in too much pain to concentrate even on the words of Scripture.

These reactions are normal—we shouldn't let them make us feel guilty or beyond hope. We are in shock. And yet we should trust that the pain will not exceed the amount we can handle. Why? Because we remain children of God, lovingly embraced even in our turmoil.

Hymn

If only my misery could be weighed,
   and all my suffering be laid on the scales!
For then it would be heavier than the sands of the sea:
   No wonder then that my words are so rash!
—Adapted from Job 6:2-3

Closing: Merciful God, give me the strength to believe that one day, in the not-too-distant future, I will find solace again. In the meantime, teach me to rest and take time to recover, so that I can acknowledge the depth of my loss.

Feeling Helpless and Vulnerable

Opening: This loss has stripped me, faithful God, and made me feel disoriented, helpless, and alone. I am overwhelmed and want to close the door and hide.

Psalm

Create in me a clean heart, O God,
    and put a new and right spirit within me. . . .
The sacrifice acceptable to God is a broken spirit;
    a broken and contrite heart, O God, you will not despise.
—Psalm 51:10, 17

Reflection

The reality of our loss, as we become more aware of it, strips away our old ways of seeing, exposes illusions toward ourselves, the world, and God. It compels us to search our heart.

And yet, strangely, it is in this helplessness that we come upon the beginning of joy. We discover that as long as we stay still the pain is not so bad and there is even a certain peace, a certain richness, a certain strength, a certain companionship that makes itself present to us when we are beaten down and lie flat with our mouths in the dust, hoping for hope.

Thomas Merton, *New Seeds of Contemplation*

Hymn

We wake up in a world not our own,
into a strange room,
struggle out of bed and
carry on with no sense of life,
bearing the weight of our helplessness—
not out of strength,
not out of hope,
but because habits remain unchanged
and we need to push on.
God help us.

Closing: Faithful God, create a new heart within this chaos; let me find a way through my brokenness and wounds. Bring me out of hiding and into the light. Let me understand that as surely as I am emptied, I will someday be filled with joy and new life.

DENIAL

Opening: May I be true to my feelings, O God, and not play a role, acting like a rock, feeling nothing, saying little. "Blessed are those who mourn, for they will be comforted" (Matthew 5:4).

PSALM

Out of the depths I cry to you, O LORD.
  Lord, hear my voice!
Let your ears be attentive
  to the voice of my supplications! . . .
My soul waits for the Lord
  more than those who watch for the morning,
  more than those who watch for the morning.
—Psalm 130:1-2, 6

REFLECTION

The temptation is to avoid responding to a loss and play the role of a stoic. When Jesus saw Mary and Martha weeping over the death of their brother, he didn't try to calm them. He didn't try to deny or take away their pain by assuring them that all would be well. Instead, he felt their grief and the grief of humankind, and wept. We weep, as well, responding to the depths of our own sorrow.

HYMN

To you, O LORD, I call;
>   my rock, do not refuse to hear me,
for if you are silent to me,
>   I shall be like those who go down to the Pit.
Hear the voice of my supplication,
>   as I cry to you for help.
—Psalm 28:1-2

Closing: May I have the faith, loving God, to walk through the pain and not deny it. You suffer with me in my grief; my heart is filled with gratitude.

Where Are You, God?

Opening: It is winter in my heart, God, and you do not respond to my utter depression and isolation. You promise no relief. You do not break the silence and turn back this bitter wind that chills me to the bone.

Psalm

My God, my God, why have you forsaken me?
Why are you so far from helping me,
from the words of my groaning?
O my God, I cry by day, but you do not answer;
and by night, but find no rest. . . .
my mouth is dried up like a potsherd,
and my tongue sticks to my jaws;
you lay me in the dust of death.
—Psalm 22:1-2, 15

Reflection

But go to Him when your need is desperate, when all other help is vain, and what do you find? A door slammed in your face, and a sound of bolting and double bolting on the inside. After that, silence. You may as well turn away. The longer you wait, the more emphatic the silence will become. . . . What can this mean? Why is He so present a commander in our time of prosperity and so very absent a help in time of trouble?

C. S. Lewis, *A Grief Observed*

Hymn

I saw no anger in God,
neither for a short time
nor for long.
For, as I see it,
if God could be angry
even for a second
we would lose
life, place, and being.
Even though we feel angry,
we are still embraced
by God's gentleness, care, and compassion.
—Adapted from Julian of Norwich, *Showings*

Closing: If only I could see a sign of hope, God, some signal to continue the journey. Your voice is at best barely audible. Fill the cold spaces of my heart with the warm announcement of your healing love.

SADNESS

Opening: Gracious God, give me strength to bear this loss in the days ahead. My heart breaks, and sadness overwhelms me.

PSALM

> Let your tears flow like a river day and night,
>   day and night;
> do not rest,
>   let yourself weep.
> Cry out at night,
>   in the early hours of darkness;
> pour your heart out like water
>   before God.
> **—Adapted from Lamentations 2:18, 19**

REFLECTION

After Lazarus died, Jesus wept. Bystanders who witnessed this realized how much Jesus loved his friend.

The pain of a loss rises up from the depths of the heart and brings us to tears. It cannot be explained, only endured. People may try to console us with the promise that time will heal. But we do not want to lose our grief, because it is bound up with our love. When grief begins to fill our heart, any attempt to divert it threatens the significance of our response.

HYMN

My dear friend,
I am glad you have come to me
in all your sadness.
I have always been with you,
and now you see my love,
and we are one,
in joy.
—Adapted from Julian of Norwich, *Showings*

Closing:
May those who sow in tears
reap with shouts of joy.
Those who go out weeping,
bearing the seed for sowing,
shall come home with shouts of joy,
carrying their sheaves.
—Psalm 126:5-6

LEARNING TO TRUST

Opening: God of compassion, teach me to trust in you. I have discovered that I can no longer control every situation. Help me believe that you have made a home in my heart and will work in my life in your own time. Teach me to rest in you untroubled as I wait for your will.

PSALM

As a deer longs for flowing streams,
> so my soul longs for you, O God. . . .
Why are you cast down, O my soul,
> and why are you disquieted within me?
Hope in God; for I shall again praise him,
> my help and my God.
—Psalm 42:1, 5-6

REFLECTION

The test comes when everything that is dear to us slips away—our home and those we love, our body and its many ways of living, our mind and its caring thoughts—and there is absolutely nothing left to hold on to. It is then that one must have the faith to surrender to a loving Lord, to believe that he will not allow us to fall into a cruel and bottomless canyon, but will bring us to the safe home which he has prepared for us.

Henri J. M. Nouwen, *In Memoriam*

HYMN

And though I suffer darknesses
In this mortal life,
That is not so hard a thing;
For though I have no light
I have the light of heaven.
For the blinder love is
The more it gives such life,
Holding the soul surrendered,
Living without light, in darkness.
**—Saint John of the Cross, "Commentary Applied to
Spiritual Things"**

Closing: God of compassion, the darkness is so great that it engulfs me entirely. But my intent is to faithfully trust in you. Trust is not easy, but even the possibility of trust becomes my guide. Show me your compassion and grace, and let me never doubt that you will help me.

PART 2
FEELING PAIN

The only way to heal pain is to feel it.

"My soul is exceedingly sorrowful, even to death."
—Adapted from Matthew 26:38

Immersed in Darkness

Opening: God, our hope, I enter the dark womb of grief and cannot escape. Let me find hope in this cavern and beginnings in this dark place. Give me the courage to take a leap of faith, to die with my loss so that I can live.

Psalm

O Lord, why do you cast me off?
     Why do you hide your face from me?
Wretched and close to death from my youth up,
     I suffer your terrors; I am desperate.
Your wrath has swept over me;
     your dread assaults destroy me.
They surround me like a flood all day long;
     from all sides they close in on me.
You have caused friend and neighbor to shun me;
     my companions are in darkness.
—**Psalm 88:14-18**

Reflection

There is wisdom in knowing that we must sometimes experience the darkness before we learn to treasure the light. Often in the loneliness of our suffering, we first realize the grace of a new life.

Faith lights the darkness even if it seems filled with death. Even with our shaken belief, we can hope for tomorrow, affirm freedom, wait for peace, and defy the forces of selfishness, fear, and cowardice. We can also pray like the father of the possessed boy in the gospel story: "I have faith. Help my lack of faith!" (adapted from Mark 9:24).

Hymn

> I said to my soul, be still,
>   and let the dark come upon you
> Which shall be the darkness of God.
> As, in a theatre,
> The lights are extinguished,
>   for the scene to be changed
> With a hollow rumble of wings,
>   with a movement of darkness on darkness.
> —T. S. Eliot, "East Coker"

Closing: You force me, God our hope, to uncover hidden strengths during a time of insecurity and powerlessness. You draw me into unknown regions, along hidden paths, so that suffering can transform me in life-giving ways.

Loss Influences All We See

Opening: God, why did you break my secure shell and throw me into a strange, threatening world? My passion for life deserts me, dreams disappear, and I walk in the shadows.

Psalm

I am like an owl of the wilderness,
    like a little owl of the waste places.
I lie awake;
    I am like a lonely bird on the housetop. . . .
For I eat ashes like bread,
    and mingle tears with my drink. . . .
[The Lord] will regard the prayer of the destitute,
    and will not despise their prayer.
—Psalm 102:6-7, 9, 17

Reflection

In our grief, loss spreads over our life like a dark cloud, influencing all that we see. No activity escapes its shadow.

We think about our loss almost all the time. It is never far from the surface of our mind when we eat, walk, fall asleep.

Daily routine no longer offers safe harbor from sadness, and our sanity seems threatened by images from the past. The specter of loss hovers over us, sapping our energy, draining our desire.

HYMN

It seemed to me
that my sorrow
exceeded death itself. . . .
Of all the pain
that leads to freedom
this is the greatest—
to see someone we love
suffer.
How could any pain be greater
than to see the person
who is all my life,
all my happiness,
and all my joy
suffer?
—Adapted from Julian of Norwich, *Showings*

Closing: Others notice my eyes glistening with tears, God, when I am trying to act as though everything is normal. I remain powerless in the face of this loss. Do not abandon me to the darkness. Help me go on, even though I have lost my way.

The Death of Dreams

Opening: I imagined the possibilities for the future; I anticipated the time we would share, the life we would create. My lost hopes and dreams cripple me, God; give me the strength to go on.

Psalm

> In the day of my trouble I seek the Lord;
>> in the night my hand is stretched out
>>> without wearying;
>> my soul refuses to be comforted.
> I think of God, and I moan;
>> I meditate, and my spirit faints.
> You keep my eyelids from closing;
>> I am so troubled that I cannot speak.
> —Psalm 77:2-4

Reflection

When a loved one dies, we not only lose the person, we lose the goals and dreams, the hope and possibilities of a future together. We realize that we will never again hear the laughter that we cherish or the loving words we have come to depend upon. We grieve what might have been different—if only. However, we can use these moments of regret to bring ourselves back to the present, to lean on what God has given us this day. We have hope that God will wipe away our tears and heal our broken hearts.

HYMN

Each day
dreams of the future
haunt me—
family gatherings,
days at the shore,
growing old together—
and the raw pain continues,
the loss of all that would be remains,
an ache gnawing in the marrow
of my bones.

Closing: God of healing, you guided me in the past; give me the strength to meet each day with hope. Though I have lost someone I love dearly, I believe that Christ came to give us eternal life so that the power of death would have no hold over us. With this belief, I cling to hope.

CRYING OUT TO GOD

Opening: Weary, worn out in body and spirit, I cry out to you, my God. My heart pours out to your compassionate presence. Release me from this suffering.

PSALM

Save me, O God,
   for the waters have come up to my neck.
I sink in deep mire,
   where there is no foothold;
I have come into deep waters,
   and the flood sweeps over me.
I am weary with my crying;
   my throat is parched.
—Psalm 69:1-3

REFLECTION

The world goes about its business as if our loss doesn't matter. Others cannot imagine our abandonment. There is no one to turn to. The ache of our heart reminds us that human life is inextricably bound up with pain. Easter seems absurd, the resurrection, impossible. Life leads to tears; love brings sorrow. We cry out. Only God can help.

Hymn

There is no end of it, the voiceless wailing,
No end to the withering of withered flowers,
To the movement of pain that is painless and motionless,
To the drift of the sea and the drifting wreckage,
The bone's prayer to Death its God.
Only the hardly, barely prayable
Prayer of the one Annunciation.
—**T. S. Eliot,** "The Dry Salvages"

Closing: The voiceless cry of my sorrow creeps up my spine and threatens to drown me, my God. Protect me; strengthen me with your love; keep me from despair. Give me confidence in your will so that I can once again experience the light and warmth of life.

Expressing Feelings

Opening: God of truth, I know that I must learn to uncover my grief and express it. Give me the strength to face my emotions honestly, to weep, to release my grief, so that I can be healed. Tears give me hope that the pain can be washed away.

Psalm

Be gracious to me, O Lord,
   for to you do I cry all day long.
Gladden the soul of your servant,
   for to you, O Lord, I lift up my soul. . . .
Give ear, O Lord, to my prayer;
   listen to my cry of supplication.
In the day of my trouble I call on you,
   for you will answer me. . . .
Teach me your way, O Lord,
   that I may walk in your truth.
—**Psalm 86:3-4, 6-7, 11**

Reflection

I took comfort in weeping in your sight over [my mother] and for her, over myself and for myself. I gave way to the tears that I had held back, so that they poured forth as much as they wished. I spread them beneath my heart, and it rested upon them, for at my heart were placed your ears, not the ears of a mere man, who would interpret with scorn my weeping.

St. Augustine, *The Confessions of St. Augustine*

HYMN

Crushed and broken,
my spirit overwhelmed,
I am unable to find the right path.
I move slowly, one foot in front of the other . . .
but this is enough.
I forge a new way
by remaining faithful to small rituals,
acting out my feelings
with long walks,
crying out,
listening to sad songs,
but
not giving up,
continuing forward
toward healing and new life.

Closing: Did you know, God of truth, how much I long to express the hurt I hide within? I know that nothing can change this devastating loss in my life, but open the door of my heart and help me heal the pain.

Ignored by Friends

Opening: Ever-present God, I feel abandoned. Even an awkward glance from a friend has the effect of a rejection. Becoming tired of my mourning, they seem to shun me in my grief. How long will I suffer this grief in my heart?

Psalm

Be gracious to me, O LORD, for I am in distress;
 my eye wastes away from grief,
 my soul and body also. . . .
I am the scorn of all my adversaries,
 a horror to my neighbors,
an object of dread to my acquaintances;
 those who see me in the street flee from me.
I have passed out of mind like one who is dead;
 I have become like a broken vessel.
—Psalm 31:9, 11-12

Reflection

Feelings of isolation are overwhelming during the stage of grief that involves feeling the pain. Some friends grow weary of our sorrow and turn away. Others offer advice that comes down to, "Snap out of it." Other people pretend not to see us and act as if our loss does not exist.

We are tempted to hide away in silence, to muffle our complaints. But wisdom teaches us to confront our feelings of alienation and to begin reinvesting our love in other people who are hurting, as well. As we look at others through the window of our grief, we will find ourselves ministering with empathy and compassion. No matter what, we need the cleansing of a free expression of our anguish.

HYMN

No man is an island, entire of itself;
every man is a piece of the continent,
a part of the main. . . .
Any man's death diminishes me
because I am involved in mankind,
and therefore never send to know
for whom the bell tolls;
it tolls for thee.
—**John Donne,** "Meditation XVII"

Closing: Answer me, ever-present God. Turn toward me, and embrace me with love. Rescue me when all my support fails. "Insults have broken my heart, so that I am in despair. I looked for pity, but there was none; and for comforters, but I found none" (Psalm 69:20).

EMOTIONAL TURMOIL

Opening: I am not resigned to this loss, God of mercy. Overwhelming feelings of anger, guilt, despair, and hope erupt in my heart, causing chaos and confusion. I am in the grasp of an anguish that controls me. Protect me so that I do not get totally lost in my feelings.

PSALM

My only food is sighs,
    and my groans pour out like water.
Whatever I fear comes true,
    whatever I dread befalls me.
For me, there is no calm, no peace;
    my torments banish rest.
—Adapted from Job 3:24-26

REFLECTION

When we turned into the road leading to our house, I suddenly felt a deep, inner sadness. Tears came to my eyes and I did not dare to look at my father. We both understood. She would not be home. She would not open the door and embrace us. She would not ask how the day had been. . . . I felt an anxious tension when my father drove into the garage and we walked up to the door. Upon entering the house it was suddenly clear to us: it had become an empty house.

Henri J. M. Nouwen, *In Memoriam*

HYMN

Ah my dear angry Lord,
Since thou dost love, yet strike;
Cast down, yet help afford;
Sure I will do the like.
I will complain, yet praise;
I will bewail, approve:
And all my sour-sweet days
I will lament, and love.
—**George Herbert,** "Bitter-Sweet"

Closing: Come near, God of mercy, and calm my inner struggle. What emotion is worth pursuing? Release me from the bonds of anger, sadness, and confusion. Let me address one feeling at a time so that I can see more clearly.

Words Offer No Comfort

Opening: God of my life, the reality of my loss makes all language seem artificial and inadequate. Words are dwarfed by my feelings. Let me find some meaning in this inexpressible, unreasonable silence.

Psalm

I am utterly spent and crushed;
  I groan because of the tumult of my heart.
O Lord, all my longing is known to you;
  my sighing is not hidden from you.
My heart throbs, my strength fails me;
  as for the light of my eyes—it also has gone from me.
My friends and companions stand aloof from my affliction,
  and my neighbors stand far off.
—Psalm 38:8-11

Reflection

The winter of grief offers no words to describe the sorrow. The mourning heart breaks in the cold silence. Tears congeal, and the lethargic soul retreats to a secret room, struck dumb with sorrow.

Why not be still and let the silence befriend us? Why not hear what we have refused to listen to, and find words that previously remained unsaid? In the depths of the heart's silence, we may begin to realize clearly that we are human and that no words will release us from our suffering.

Hymn

> A grief without a pang, void, dark, and drear,
>   A stifled, drowsy, unimpassioned grief,
>   Which finds no natural outlet, no relief,
>   In word, or sigh, or tear—
> —**Samuel Taylor Coleridge**, "Dejection"

Closing: I desperately search for answers in this awesome stillness, God of my life. Where can I find direction except from you? To you I look for support. "God is good to those who wait in trust, to the soul that searches for divine relief. Waiting patiently for God to save us will be rewarded" (adapted from Lamentations 3:25-26).

The Transience of Life

Opening: Loving God, I am fearful because I sense that my life is quickly ending. Give me the strength to fight the pull of hopelessness. Help me grow to accept my mortality.

Psalm

"LORD, let me know my end,
　　and what is the measure of my days;
　　let me know how fleeting my life is.
You have made my days a few handbreadths,
　　and my lifetime is as nothing in your sight.
Surely everyone stands as a mere breath.
Surely everyone goes about like a shadow.
Surely for nothing they are in turmoil;
　　they heap up, and do not know who will gather."
—Psalm 39:4-6

Reflection

After a painful loss, we may awaken abruptly in the middle of the night feeling the quick passage of time. The sound of a branch clicking against the roof, the rhythm of the clock, the drip in the bathroom sink mark each escaping moment.

Years have faded into whispers barely audible in the thick night silence. We know that we will rise in the morning barely remembering these twilight visions. Yet, we might feel the need to stop during the day, glance through a window, and remind ourselves to relish the mystery of our life.

HYMN

Gather ye rosebuds while ye may,
   Old Time is still a-flying;
And the same flower that smiles today
   Tomorrow will be dying.
The glorious lamp of heaven, the sun,
   The higher he's a-getting,
The sooner will his race be run,
   And nearer he's to setting.
—**Robert Herrick**, "To the Virgins to Make Much of Time"

Closing: Awareness of my fragility, compassionate God, threatens to deaden my spirit and take the effort out of my work. Teach me to enjoy the beauty of each day and celebrate life's sacred moments: "Teach us to count our days that we may gain a wise heart" (Psalm 90:12).

HUMILITY

Opening: Saving God, you have shaken my secure ground. I never thought I could lose control. Will I drown in this dark abyss? Will you save me? I can no longer save myself. Help me!

PSALM

> O LORD, my heart is not lifted up,
> 　my eyes are not raised too high;
> I do not occupy myself with things
> 　too great and too marvelous for me.
> But I have calmed and quieted my soul,
> 　like a weaned child with its mother;
> 　my soul is like the weaned child that is with me.
> —Psalm 131:1-2

REFLECTION

God draws close to those whose spirit is crushed and whose courage is broken (adapted from Psalm 34:18). We lose control, fall to our knees, but our humiliation is not a punishment. It is a call to wake up.

When our loss teaches us that we cannot control life, a surprising thing happens: we are able to hear God's answer to our suffering. God speaks, and we are invited to respond with our entire being. Stripped of the illusion of our control, we are graced with an awareness of what is truly important.

Hymn

Weak and fearful, I ask,
   where is my true strength?
Drowning in dark water,
   where is my rescuer?
Crushed by loss,
   where is my savior?
My heart aches,
   my efforts fail.
Come near, O God,
   strengthen, rescue, save me.
Praise to you, O Holy One!

Closing: Saving God, when all else fails, I turn to you. You are the horizon beyond all other horizons, the final net that catches me. Teach me the path of true humility so that I can learn to share in your strength and love.

Hear My Prayer

Opening: In this time of desperate need, when all resources have failed, hear my prayer, gracious God. Give comfort to my failing spirit.

Psalm

Hear my prayer, O Lord;
>   let my cry come to you.
Do not hide your face from me
>   in the day of my distress.
Incline your ear to me;
>   answer me speedily in the day when I call.
For my days pass away like smoke,
>   and my bones burn like a furnace.
My heart is stricken and withered like grass;
>   I am too wasted to eat my bread.
—Psalm 102:1-4

Reflection

We storm heaven with the cries of our heart. It is difficult to say prayers, but we let our hearts speak up with raw feeling; bewilderment, sadness, or rage. Often we consider our prayers to be unheard, unanswered, only to find small, brief, signs of hope, laser-like rays of light slicing through the darkness, giving us courage to face another day.

Hymn

"Ask, and it will be given you;
search, and you will find;
knock, and the door will be opened for you.
For everyone who asks receives,
and everyone who searches finds,
and for everyone who knocks,
the door will be opened."
—Luke 11:9-10

Closing: God of mystery, teach me to open my heart to you like the psalmist who persisted in his prayer, confident that the Lord would come to his aid. "Incline your ear, O Lord, and answer me, for I am poor and needy. . . . You are my God; be gracious to me, O Lord, for to you do I cry all day long" (Psalm 86:1, 2-3).

Praying Through
Our Losses

PART 3
HEALING

If we continue to struggle through the painful times,
even though progress seems minimal,
we uncover an inner strength
and realize what is truly important in life.

We also boast in our sufferings, knowing that suffering produces endurance, and endurance produces character, and character produces hope, and hope does not disappoint us, because God's love has been poured into our hearts through the Holy Spirit. . . .

—Romans 5:3-5

RECOVERY

Opening: My heart has been a desert, God of love; spiritual starvation threatens me. Bring me to the place where water flows, where your gentle and generous hands can repair my spirit.

PSALM

I remember the days of old,
    I think about all your deeds,
    I meditate on the works of your hands.
I stretch out my hands to you;
    my soul thirsts for you like a parched land.
Answer me quickly, O LORD;
    my spirit fails;
Do not hide your face from me,
    or I shall be like those who go down to the Pit.
Let me hear of your steadfast love in the morning,
    for in you I put my trust.
Teach me the way I should go,
    for to you I lift up my soul.
—Psalm 143:5-8

REFLECTION

Though we may wish that healing could be granted by another, it is a process that we ourselves must embrace. Healing is a deep spring within us that we uncover in our own time and in our own way. We may continue to struggle with fear and pain, but we know that, in the midst of suffering, we must affirm life. A divine hand has been reaching for us all along. Now we are ready to receive it and let it enrich our soul, allowing love to grow.

HYMN

In the terrible dryness
   of my heart,
create in me
   a quiet oasis;
in this bitter and thirsty land,
   this treeless ocean of sand,
refresh my spirit and open my weak hands
   to the gift of your love.

Closing:
   When the poor and needy seek water,
      and there is none,
      and their tongue is parched with thirst,
   I the LORD will answer them. . . .
   I will make the wilderness a pool of water,
      and the dry land springs of water.
   —Isaiah 41:17, 18

Putting Life Back in Order

Opening: Merciful God, facing my loss has changed me and made me discover what is really important in my life. Gaining a new perspective has lessened the pain and deepened the sadness. But I am ready to move forward.

Psalm

All this has come upon us,
    yet we have not forgotten you,
    or been false to your covenant.
Our heart has not turned back,
    nor have our steps departed from your way.
—Psalm 44:17-18

Reflection

It is time to accept God's promise and embrace the new—though perhaps unwelcome—changes in our life. We need to return to work, establish manageable goals, rededicate ourselves to the routine tasks of daily living. Life is not over—we know this. Decisions need to be made so that we can now move on.

Coping with the new situations we encounter as we return to normal life challenges our resources. We might be more comfortable remaining at home with our grief. Our loss is special, and most other people probably don't understand how great it is. Yet we know that we must also allow normalcy to return. We must remember the blessings of our life.

HYMN

Sadness is my garden
   where cold blossoms grow,
   yet winter passes into spring.
For months now,
   I have lived with weeping,
   bare thickets, and long evenings.
But someone told me
   that at the edge of the woods
   she saw white flowers growing.
I want to go there
   and touch a place in my heart
   where dreams can refresh
   and days grow green with promise.

Closing: Merciful God, I am emerging from the darkness—enough to see the need for transformation and to venture into a new, unpredictable world. No one leaves behind the darkness without suffering and pain. Give me the strength to believe in my life again. Give me confidence and hope. Today is the time for healing.

Morning Dread

Opening: I dread the mornings, O God. I used to awaken to a dawn filled with possibilities, hopes, and shared dreams; now I am greeted by the cruel reality of spending another day without the one I loved so dearly.

Psalm

The cords of death encompassed me;
  the torrents of perdition assailed me. . . .
In my distress I called upon the LORD;
  to my God I cried for help.
From his temple he heard my voice,
  and my cry to him reached his ears.
—**Psalm 18:4, 6**

Reflection

The silent house, the empty chair, the absence of greetings, the lost routines; mornings remind us of all we are missing. Usually it is the small things we miss the most, the little rituals that make up life together. Waking up each morning, remembering the absence, it seems that the person we loved dies over and over again. Yet, God is aware of our pain and dread. Remembering God's goodness and faithfulness this day, we cry out with an expectant heart, and hand over our tormented lives. God will be our refuge.

HYMN

Mornings
we reawaken
to a different world;
everything is changed
forever.
We sort out our lives
into manageable piles,
walking through the house
aware that
"our" life
has become
"my" life.

Closing: Faithful God, I cry out for deliverance, remaining hopeful because your love will never fail me. "I will sing of your might; I will sing aloud of your steadfast love in the morning. For you have been a fortress for me and a refuge in the day of my distress" (Psalm 59:16).

FORGIVE YOURSELF

Opening: O God, I regret the thoughtless words and painful times. I ask myself, was there something I should have done or something I should have said to make things better between us? Grieving has become complex and riddled with guilt. How can I bear it?

PSALM

Let all who are faithful
 offer prayer to you;
at a time of distress, the rush of mighty waters
 shall not reach them.
You are a hiding place for me;
 you preserve me from trouble;
 you surround me with glad cries of deliverance.
—Psalm 32:6-7

REFLECTION

Self-recrimination seems inevitable with grieving. We question ourselves repeatedly: Why didn't I say "I love you" more often? Should I have paid more attention? Should I have visited more often? Could I have prevented this death somehow by reacting more quickly or taking her/him to the hospital sooner? It is so easy to condemn ourselves when these negative thoughts fill our minds. Yet to keep the memory of our loved one truthful, we must recall the positive memories as well as the negative ones;

we must forgive ourselves and accept the forgiveness that God makes available to us through the death of Jesus Christ.

HYMN

So much left unsaid,
telling her that she failed me,
the guilt at being angry
with her,
I decide
that some things
are better left unsaid.
Even saying "I love you"
is difficult,
a history of resentment
rises up,
but in my heart,
the "I love you"
echoes
putting all else in perspective.

Closing: In my weakness I may have failed this relationship; but what is important is that I loved and will continue to love, in all my fragility and my weakness. Help me, loving and merciful God.

LEARNING PATIENCE

Opening: God of love, teach me patience. Let me wait to hear your counsel. I was in a hurry to have the pain taken away, to have you fulfill my plans. But now I wait, yearning for light to dispel the darkness. I wait to respond to your wisdom, which always leads to wholeness.

PSALM

Do not let those who wait for you be put to shame;
    let them be ashamed who are wantonly treacherous.
Make me to know your ways, O LORD;
    teach me your paths.
Lead me in your truth, and teach me,
    for you are the God of my salvation;
    for you I wait all day long.
—**Psalm 25:3-5**

REFLECTION

We are not the same after the experience of loss. Grief has provided us with an opportunity to discover our deepest character and to reconsider what is most important in our life.

Grieving is an advent in our life, a time of waiting, a time of yearning for light. We long for a place of inner peace, a secure home within. We no longer want to be strangers to ourselves and to others. Guide us home, God of light.

Hymn

I said to my soul, be still, and wait without hope
For hope would be hope for the wrong thing;
   wait without love
For love would be love of the wrong thing;
   there is yet faith
But the faith and the love and the hope are all
   in the waiting.
Wait without thought, for you are not ready for thought:
So the darkness shall be the light, and the
   stillness the dancing.
—T. S. Eliot, "East Coker"

Closing: God of love, lead me out of lonely exile and let me glimpse the homeland. You are the God of all those who wander in darkness. You are the home that my soul cries out for. Grant me the strength and patience to meet the days to come in the joyful expectation of a new life with those I love.

Be Gentle with Yourself

Opening: Holy Friend, it is time to rest more deeply in your care. I need to lie fallow like a plot of land left unseeded, so that my heart can once again bear riches. Show me how to be kind to myself and not to worry.

Psalm

The Lord is my shepherd, I shall not want.
　　He makes me lie down in green pastures;
he leads me beside still waters;
　　he restores my soul. . . .
Even though I walk through the darkest valley,
　　I fear no evil;
for you are with me. . . .
Surely goodness and mercy shall follow me
　　all the days of my life,
and I shall dwell in the house of the Lord
　　my whole life long.
—Psalm 23:1-3, 4, 6

Reflection

"You have survived the winter because you are, and were, and always will be very much loved," said the sun. "For that small place deep within you that remained unfrozen and open to mystery, that is where I have made my dwelling. And long, long before you felt my warmth surrounding you, you were being freed and formed from within in ways so deep and profound that you could not possibly know what was happening."

Mary Fahy, *The Tree That Survived the Winter*

HYMN

And God said . . .
"Does a woman forget the baby at her breast,
    or fail to cherish her own child?
Yet even if some do forget,
    I will never forget you.
You are etched in the palm of my hand.
In your heart you will wonder,
    Who has given me these gifts?
I was empty and barren,
    who nourished me?
When I was all alone
    who stayed with me?"
And God said . . .
"Those who hope in me will never be abandoned."
—Adapted from Isaiah 49:15-16, 21, 25

Closing: Holy Friend, I remember a time when my heart became frozen winter soil, unable to bear any growth. Now I open myself to receive your nourishing rain and warming sun. Thank you for nurturing me and giving me the opportunity to flourish.

A Childlike Vision

Opening: Holy Light, grief has given me some clarity of vision. I see my life differently, with more depth and compassion. Grant me the wisdom to stand before the mystery of all life, free in spirit like a child.

Psalm

One thing I asked of the Lord,
    that will I seek after:
to live in the house of the Lord
    all the days of my life,
to behold the beauty of the Lord,
    and to inquire in his temple. . . .
I believe that I shall see the goodness of the Lord
    in the land of the living.
—Psalm 27:4, 13

Reflection

Even in the midst of grief and loss, we might try to depend on rational thinking and seek to control our life. Further along the journey of recovery from loss, we are less likely to attempt to make sense out of everything. We learn the hard lesson that no explanation truly satisfies.

With a fresh sense of our dependence on God, we might start to feel like children again, aware of the small mysteries around us. We don't want to lose touch with the giftedness of our life, and so we might imagine ourselves as children in Jesus' loving embrace: "'Let the little children come to me; . . . for it is to such as these that the kingdom of God belongs'" (Mark 10:14).

HYMN

Once you have
the joy of a child,
it lasts forever
like a dream,
always alive
though buried in adult days
under hurt, losses, and insecurity;
but it rises again,
an island of light
resurrected
in a dark ocean,
when you are struck down
with the weight of grief
and your eyes are opened.

> "Whoever welcomes this child
> in my name welcomes me. . ." (Luke 9:48).

Closing: May I continue to wonder, God of light, and never stifle my childlike awe at your gifts. After being shocked by pain, I want to be open to mystery in a new, unexpected way. Grace me with ears to hear the song of the universe and eyes to see the light. You invite me to this cosmic dance.

The Fear of Letting Go

Opening: God of power, give me the strength to make decisions and to gently let go of the part of me that is still holding on to grief. The time has come to release the pain. Life is not over. Although it will never be the same, it can once again be full.

Psalm

For you, O God, have tested us;
    you have tried us as silver is tried.
You brought us into the net;
    you laid burdens on our backs; . . .
    we went through fire and through water;
yet you have brought us out to a spacious place.
I will come into your house with burnt offerings;
    I will pay you my vows,
those that my lips uttered
    and my mouth promised when I was in trouble.
—Psalm 66:10-11, 12-14

Reflection

We fear letting go, yet life is a continual process of letting go. Each choice we make entails the loss of other possibilities. We let go of dreams, youth, health, friends, loved ones, and eventually our own life.

Letting go of grief can be the greatest challenge as we mourn. Grief can become a substitute for whomever or whatever we lost.

Letting go and feeling better can be perceived as the betrayal of our memory of the loss. Grieving beyond our time, however, threatens our own aliveness.

Letting go hastens our transformation. By surrendering our loss with faith and hope, our exhausted heart can choose new life.

Hymn

I am not ready to die,
But I am learning to trust death
As I have trusted life.
I am moving
Toward a new freedom
Born of detachment,
And a sweeter grace—
Learning to let go.
—**May Sarton,** "Gestalt at Sixty"

Closing: God of power, letting go challenges me to trust you when the sky is still mostly dark. May Jesus, who lost everything but was transformed with Easter life, remind me of your abiding love for me.

A Believing Heart

Opening: At times I have felt that death has overcome God, that at the time of my loss God didn't care or was just powerless. God of mystery, help me in my struggle with confusion and resentment toward you.

Psalm

Gracious is the Lord, and righteous;
  our God is merciful.
The Lord protects the simple;
  when I was brought low, he saved me.
Return, O my soul, to your rest,
  for the Lord has dealt bountifully with you.
For you have delivered my soul from death,
  my eyes from tears,
  my feet from stumbling.
I walk before the Lord
  in the land of the living.
—Psalm 116:5-9

Reflection

Those who first heard these words of hope, "In the world you face persecution, but take courage; I have conquered the world!" (see John: 16:33), must have felt elated; yet, a short time later, these same men were overwhelmed with hopelessness. They witnessed the one they followed, Christ, seemingly conquered by death. With grief still fresh, we may also feel times of despair, yet we can also believe that all this pain is redeemed by God. This pain can become useful, something from which we can learn—if not today, then sometime in the future.

HYMN

Jesus prayed
that a cup of suffering
would be removed.
It was not.
He drank it
and followed it
to the cross of love,
where we are saved,
rescued,
made whole,
in and through his love.

Closing: The apostle Paul reminds us that glory awaits those who hope in God. He says, "I consider that the sufferings of this present time are not worth comparing with the glory about to be revealed to us" (Romans 8:18). Even though the pain continues to haunt me, let me understand, God of all hope, that this pain—this life—is but a single moment in the scope of eternity.

Loving Again

Opening: God of love, you shelter me in your embrace. In the face of sadness and despair, you place invitations to love again in my path. In my heart I realize that even when my feelings were most intense and the abyss most threatening, a yes to life was rising in my soul.

Psalm

If the Lord had not been my help,
  my soul would soon have lived in the land of silence.
When I thought, "My foot is slipping,"
  your steadfast love, O Lord, held me up.
When the cares of my heart are many,
  your consolations cheer my soul.
—Psalm 94:17-19

Reflection

While we are grieving, we think that we will never love again. The pain of our broken heart can tempt us to desire a heart of stone, a heart invulnerable to the suffering of loss.

Yet God, like a compassionate parent, watches over us, waiting with us, surrounding us with faithful love. God's love does not take away our pain, but God, our faithful companion, will always remain with us in spite of any loss. Gradually, as we heal, we will cherish love more dearly and try to live each day as if it were our last.

HYMN

Come then, my love,
   my lovely one, come.
For see, winter is past,
   the rains are over and gone.
The flowers appear on the earth.
   The season of glad songs has come.
Come then, my love,
   my lovely one, come.
Show me your face,
   let me hear your voice.
—Adapted from Song of Solomon 2:10-14

Closing: God of love, how good it is to feel your gentle presence and life-giving energy. Thank you for creating me in the image of love and watching over me with tenderness and compassion. You are "near to the brokenhearted, and . . . the crushed in spirit" (Psalm 34:18).

God's Faithfulness

Opening: Faithful God, there are times when I am sure that I will never again feel anything but sorrow. Take my suffering and make my life an offering to you.

Psalm

You who have made me see many troubles and calamities
    will revive me again;
from the depths of the earth
    you will bring me up again.
You will increase my honor
    and comfort me once again.
I will also praise you with the harp
    for your faithfulness, O my God;
I will sing praises to you with the lyre.
—Psalm 71:20-22

Reflection

I once saw a stonecutter remove great pieces from a huge rock on which he was working. In my imagination I thought, *That rock must be hurting terribly. Why does this man wound the rock so much?* But as I looked longer, I saw the figure of a graceful dancer emerge gradually from the stone, looking at me in my mind's eye and saying, "You foolish man, didn't you know that I had to suffer and thus enter into my glory?" The mystery of the dance is that its movements are discovered in the mourning.

Henri J. M. Nouwen, *Turn My Mourning into Dancing*

Hymn

This is what we have heard from him
    and proclaim to you:
God is light, and there is no darkness in God at all.
—Adapted from 1 John 1:5

Closing: Faithful and patient God, I will continue to call to you through my pain, and in spite of my pain. Some day in the future I will be grateful for your patient and consistent call. Give me the strength to answer; take my hand and lead me.

PART 4
NEW LIFE

Loss changes our vision of life;
it can give birth to deeper self-awareness
and open our heart to greater love
for other people and for God.

You should carry each other's troubles.

—Adapted from Galatians 6:2

DELIVERED FROM DARKNESS

Opening: Looking at the stars in the night sky, I am reminded that your deliverance, faithful God, is always near, always in the process of coming to fulfillment. The mystery of light on the horizon grows and guides me through these times of trouble.

PSALM

Some sat in darkness and in gloom,
    prisoners in misery and in irons. . . .
Then they cried to the LORD in their trouble,
    and he saved them from their distress;
he brought them out of darkness and gloom,
    and broke their bonds asunder.
—Psalm 107:10, 13-14

REFLECTION

In a last violent protest against the hopelessness of imminent death, I sensed my spirit piercing through the enveloping gloom. I felt it transcend that hopeless, meaningless world, and from somewhere I heard a victorious "Yes" in answer to my question of the existence of an ultimate purpose. At that moment a light was lit in a distant farmhouse, which stood on the horizon as if painted there, in the midst of the miserable grey of a dawning morning.

Viktor E. Frankl, *Man's Search for Meaning*

Hymn

Then I saw a new heaven and a new earth. I saw the holy city, the new Jerusalem, coming down out of heaven from God, prepared as a bride dressed for her husband.

"Look, here God lives among human beings.
God will wipe away all the tears from their eyes;
there will be no more death,
and no more mourning and sadness or pain.
The world of the past has gone.

"The city did not need the sun or the moon for light,
since it was lit by the radiant glory of God."
—Adapted from Revelation 21:1-4, 23

Closing: Faithful God, I am not troubled by the night. Winter turns to spring. Resurrection swallows up death. I do not worry about the city of today, but yearn for your reign in the eternity of tomorrow.

HOPE

Opening: I hope in you, holy One, although at times there seemed to be no reason for hope. In loneliness and suffering, I have unlocked the door where hope hides and have quietly embraced your promises. I sing songs to you because you offered me hope when despair stalked and threatened me.

PSALM

For you, O Lord, are my hope,
   my trust, O LORD, from my youth.
Upon you I have leaned from my birth;
   it was you who took me from my mother's womb.
My praise is continually of you. . . .
You who have made me see many troubles and calamities
   will revive me again;
from the depths of the earth you will bring me up again. . . .
I will also praise you with the harp
   for your faithfulness, O my God;
I will sing praises to you with the lyre,
   O Holy One of Israel.
—**Psalm 71:5-6, 20, 22**

REFLECTION

Nothing, not even death, separates a hopeful person from God. So strong is hope that some hold on to it even at the center of chaos and imminent death. Sometimes, when we are overcome with hopelessness, we discover an unexpected light deep inside, beyond the conscious mind. We believe that there is an answer, if only we have enough patience to wait for it to be revealed to us. Our own plans fail us, so we live on hope, believing as Paul did that nothing already in existence and nothing still to come . . . will be able to come between us and the love of God, known to us in Christ Jesus (adapted from Romans 8:38-39).

HYMN

    Grief melts away
    Like snow in May,
As if there were no such cold thing.

    Who would have thought my shriveled heart
Could have recovered greenness? It was gone
    quite underground; as flowers depart
To see their mother-root, when they have blown;
    Where they together
    All the hard weather,
    Dead to the world, keep house unknown.
—**George Herbert,** "The Flower"

Closing: Let me breathe the air of hope, holy One. Even though I question everything and sometimes let my expectations get in the way, let me never lose hope. Because my suffering has made me vulnerable, I embrace hope more than ever. Fill me with joy and peace through the power of your Spirit.

Sensitive to the Mystery of Life

Opening: God of compassion, I am no longer looking for an explanation for this loss and have become aware of the horizons beyond my limited mind. Keep me open to the awesome mystery that surrounds my life.

Psalm

O LORD, you have searched me and known me.
You know when I sit down and when I rise up;
    you discern my thoughts from far away.
You search out my path and my lying down,
    and are acquainted with all my ways. . . .
For it was you who formed my inward parts;
    you knit me together in my mother's womb.
I praise you, for I am fearfully and wonderfully made.
    Wonderful are your works;
that I know very well.
—Psalm 139:1-3, 13-14

Reflection

No loss is so great that it eliminates the fact that our lives are mystery and that experience and thought, emotion and free will, love and reason will prevail in time.

Things that go wrong or the onslaught of suffering from a loss do not threaten us as much as forgetting the potential of what life can become. The usual boundaries around the self collapse under the weight of a loss, and once again we stand in wonder at one fact: we exist. God invites us to say yes to life.

Hymn

"God thunders wondrously with his voice;
    he does great things that we cannot comprehend.
For to the snow he says, 'Fall on the earth';
    and the shower of rain, his heavy shower of rain,
serves as a sign on everyone's hand,
    so that all whom he has made may know it. . . .
"Hear this, O Job;
    stop and consider the wondrous works of God."
—Job 37:5-7, 14

Closing: God of compassion, encountering mystery humbles and frees me at the same time. Let me never take for granted the force of love, the power of tenderness, the warmth of touch, the presence of another, the revelation of suffering. Make my life an empty vessel waiting to be filled; open my hands so that I am always ready to receive.

Loss Opens to Grace

Opening: Gracious God, you blessed me with the opportunity to experience new life rising out of the abyss of grief. Give me the strength to bear this process of spiritual death and rebirth, and let me gain wisdom from it.

Psalm

O LORD my God, I cried to you for help,
and you have healed me.
O LORD, you brought up my soul from Sheol,
restored me to life from among those
gone down to the Pit. . . .
For his anger is but for a moment;
his favor is for a lifetime.
Weeping may linger for the night,
but joy comes with the morning.
—Psalm 30:2-3, 5

Reflection

We cry ourselves to sleep at night but wake up to sunrise and grace in the morning. Through loss we experience a spiritual death while still alive. This process seems cruel, but Jesus said it was necessary: the old self needs to die so that a new person can come to life. Good Friday eventually culminates in Easter.

Grieving offers us an opportunity for a new vision. Our loss may diminish our tolerance for old values. Old pleasures may no longer satisfy. Instead we might find unexpected joy in ordinary gestures of love and previously unnoticed expressions of beauty. We can grow increasingly grateful for the goodness without and within and believe that we are truly precious in God's eyes.

HYMN

Rise heart; thy Lord is risen. Sing his praise
  Without delays,
Who takes thee by the hand, that thou likewise
  With him mayst rise.
—**George Herbert**, "Easter"

Closing: Gracious God, your ways are mystery. Let me see my grief as a divine gift that offers me a new appreciation for my life and for what is truly important. Keep me awake so that I never take my life for granted and lose the ability to cherish all that I am given.

STRENGTH

Opening: I have learned, gracious God, to find my strength in you. Remain at my side as I make my way through the days ahead. Help me remain true to myself and my feelings.

PSALM

> For God alone my soul waits in silence,
>   for my hope is from him.
> He alone is my rock and my salvation,
>   my fortress; I shall not be shaken.
> On God rests my deliverance and my honor;
>   my mighty rock, my refuge is in God.
> Trust in him at all times, O people;
>   pour out your heart before him;
>   God is a refuge for us.
> —Psalm 62:5-8

REFLECTION

Turning to God as a "refuge" is not a prayer that eliminates grieving once and for all. Even though we are gaining new strength to go on, grief continues to rise unexpectedly to the surface. If we are true to ourselves and our feelings, we won't hide this grief or expect God to completely eradicate it. At times like these, we need to rely on God's goodness and strength. As a result, we can use times of sadness to bring us closer to God.

We find faith *through* the mysterious ways of grief, not in spite of them.

Hymn

> Indeed O God, you yourself are my lamp,
>   You light up my darkness.
> For who is God but Yahweh,
>   who is a rock but our God:
> this God who fills me with strength?
>   **—Adapted from 2 Samuel 22:29, 32-33**

Closing: God, my Rock, I realize that nothing can deprive me of divine strength. You answer my prayer, drawing me toward the fire of your life, providing me with strength, security, and salvation. Gusts of wind continue to howl around me, but I pass through safely with the security you provide.

Reclaiming Joy and
a Sense of Humor

Opening: Holy Friend, let me laugh and find joy even while I suffer, so that I can find inner peace and put my loss in perspective. Let me praise you and proclaim your goodness.

Psalm

You have turned my mourning into dancing;
    you have taken off my sackcloth
    and clothed me with joy,
so that my soul may praise you and not be silent.
    O Lord my God, I will give thanks to you forever.
—Psalm 30:11-12

Reflection

If we have faith that God is already present in the world guiding us toward salvation, laughing and crying with us, then we can discover joy even in the profoundest grief.

Our recovery from grief may begin with a half-smile at a witty remark. With grace, we may soon laugh at life's many ironies. The gift of humor provides an antidote to unremitting seriousness.

God truly cares for us. We can let go of our efforts to control the universe. The Creator wants us fully alive, fully joyous.

Hymn

Yahweh, your God, is in your midst,
   renewing you with love;
dancing with shouts of joy for you
   as on a day of festival.
—Adapted from Zephaniah 3:17-18

Closing: Holy Friend, join my heart with your joyful song. Set me free from anxieties that only isolate me, fears that stifle my song, and emptiness that saps my energy. Let laughter, dance, and song be my path to balance and peace.

Reaching Out to Others

Opening: Loving Companion, I can no longer remain separate. I want to love again. Knowing that you will not abandon me reinforces my desire to love. I trust you to sustain me as I try to reach out. Fill me with the energy of hope.

Psalm

Sing to him a new song;
 play skillfully on the strings, with loud shouts.
For the word of the LORD is upright,
 and all his work is done in faithfulness.
He loves righteousness and justice;
 the earth is full of the steadfast love of the LORD.
—Psalm 33:3-5

Reflection

Healing grief has the power to enlarge our capacity to empathize with the suffering of others. Confronting our own loneliness, sorrow, and suffering invites us to care for other people, people like us.

When we grieve and let go, loss can make us better people. In the final stage of grief, the desire for loving relationships makes a tentative return once again. We might find ourselves more vulnerable to love and willing to risk loving.

If grief deepens our faith, hope, and willingness to love, then death and loss, small or great, cannot win.

Hymn

Love is as powerful as death. . . .
Love's lightning blazes with fire,
   the very fire of God.
No torrent can drown the fires of love.
—Adapted from Song of Solomon 8:6-7

Closing: Loving Companion, give me the strength to comfort others, as you have comforted me. Let me weep with those who weep and share the anguish and pain of those that you call me to help. Let me be a sign of your love. Move me to love again.

PILGRIM WAYS

Opening: God, my guide, as a pilgrim I feel far from home and yearn to be delivered once and for all from isolation, loss, and suffering. Light my way, and let me rest in a place of peace. You once promised, "I shall bring you back to the place from which I exiled you" (adapted from Jeremiah 29:14). Grief has been exile. I am ready for you to lead me home.

PSALM

Happy are those whose strength is in you,
in whose heart are the highways to Zion.
As they go through the valley of Baca
they make it a place of springs;
the early rain also covers it with pools. . . .
For the LORD God is a sun and shield;
he bestows favor and honor.
—Psalm 84:5-6, 11

REFLECTION

Grief intensifies the awareness of ourselves as pilgrims who will never fully reach our goal of union with others and God in this life. We are exiles, searching for home.

God, however, welcomes those who are pilgrims and brings hope to all those who have discovered that they are homeless. God is present not only at the end of the journey, but all along the way. Even as we travel toward God, our divine guide journeys with us, a bright star directing us through dark nights.

If we listen and are attentive to the love and hope that we offer each other, we will experience his intimacy and support.

HYMN

Through many dangers, toils, and snares
    I have already come;
It's grace that brought me safe thus far,
    and grace will lead me home.
How sweet the name of Jesus sounds
    to a true believer's ear.
It soothes his sorrows and heals his wounds,
    and drives away his tears.
—**John Newton,** "Amazing Grace"

Closing: God, my guide, take my hand and lead me through my suffering to your love and justice, peace and freedom. May I sing and dance, joyful in your embrace.

Risen Life

Opening: O God, you are the only one who can help me grow through my grief, the only one who has the power to heal the wound from my loss.

Psalm

> God is our refuge and strength,
>> a very present help in trouble.
> Therefore we will not fear, though the earth should change,
>> though the mountains shake in the heart of the sea. . . .
> "Be still, and know that I am God!
>> I am exalted among the nations,
>> I am exalted in the earth."
> —Psalm 46:1-2, 10

Reflection

Though our grief is still real, we need not despair. We have hope based on the reality of the resurrection. The presence of the Holy Spirit in our lives assures us of our future in eternity. We shall not perish (see John 10:28), and we will meet our loved ones in heaven on the day of redemption. Those who have come before give witness that God is faithful and true, "our refuge and strength" (Psalm 46:1).

HYMN

Do not let your hearts be troubled.
   I am going now to prepare a place for you,
and after I have gone and prepared you a place,
   I shall return to take you to myself.
You know the way to the place where I am going.
—Adapted from John 14:1, 3-4

Closing: We turn to God in this time of mourning and find ourselves saying, along with the psalmist, "I shall not die; but I shall live" (Psalm 118:17).

Afterword

For everything there is a season, and a time for every matter
under heaven:
a time to be born, and a time to die;
a time to plant, and a time to pluck up what is planted;
a time to kill, and a time to heal;
a time to break down, and a time to build up;
a time to weep, and a time to laugh;
a time to mourn, and a time to dance;
a time to throw away stones,
   and a time to gather stones together;
a time to embrace, and a time to refrain from embracing;
a time to seek, and a time to lose;
a time to keep, and a time to throw away;
a time to tear, and a time to sew;
a time to keep silence, and a time to speak. . . .
He [God] has made everything suitable for its time.

—Ecclesiastes 3:1-7, 11

ACKNOWLEDGMENTS

Unless otherwise noted, Scripture passages are from the New Revised Standard Version Bible: Catholic Edition, copyright © 1989, 1993 Division of Christian Education of the National Council of the Churches of Christ in the United States. All rights reserved. Used with permission.

Scriptural material cited as "adapted from" is freely adapted and is not to be understood or used as official translations of the Bible.

The excerpt by Saint Augustine is from *The Confessions of St. Augustine,* translated by John K. Ryan (Garden City, NY: Image Books, 1960), p. 226. Copyright © 1960 by Doubleday and Company.

The excerpt by Samuel Taylor Coleridge is from *The Portable Coleridge,* edited by I. A. Richards (New York: Viking Press, 1961), p. 170. Copyright © 1950 by Viking Press.

The excerpt by John Donne is from *The Norton Anthology of English Literature,* 4th ed., vol. 1, edited by M. H. Abrams (New York: W. W. Norton and Co., 1979), pp. 1108–09. Copyright © 1979 by W. W. Norton and Company.

Excerpts by T. S. Eliot from "East Coker" in *Four Quartets,* US copyright © 1940 by T. S. Eliot and renewed 1968 by Esme Val-